I0107448

HOW TO BE A GOOD OJOOSAN

How to Be a Good Ojoosan

Tammie Oka

Kahuaomānoa Press
Honolulu, Hawai'i

Copyright © 2008 by Tammie Oka

All Rights Reserved

Printed in Hawai'i

~Kahuaomānoa Press~

President & Chief Editor	Brandy Nālani McDougall
Vice-President & Managing Editor	Ann Inoshita
Associate Editor & Treasurer	Ryan Oishi
Assistant Editors	Kai Gaspar,
	Bryan Kamaoli Kuwada,
	Aiko Yamashiro
Faculty Advisor	Robert Sullivan
Typesetting & Book Design	Brent Fujinaka

Cover photograph is of the author as a child posing behind a life-size cut-out at a children's museum. Cover photograph and section sketches courtesy of the author.

Kahuaomānoa means, in ʻōlelo Hawaiʻi, "the fruit of Mānoa" and "foundation of Mānoa."

Kahuaomānoa Press is dedicated toward the publication and promotion of excellence in student art and literature. As such, every effort is made to privilege the student voice and perspective first and foremost.

Acknowledgements

Thank you to the staff at Kahuaomānoa Press: Brandy, Ann, Ryan, Kai, Aiko, Bryan, and Brent. This book would not have been possible without your support and guidance.

I am appreciative toward all my mentors in the English Department. Thank you to Robert Sullivan. He taught me to stop rhyming my words and to write with emotion. Without his encouragement, most of these poems would remain lost on my hard drive. I am also grateful to Albert Wendt for always creating a nurturing writing environment.

Thank you to the poets at Squaw Valley. Never in a million years would I have imagined that I'd get to meet my favorite poet, let alone workshop with her.

Special thanks to those who have lent an ear over the years. Thanks to Estelle and Jen for always picking up the phone no matter what hour. Mom, thank you for allowing me to write with freedom. Dad, thank you for supporting me through college.

Everyone has a great storyteller in their family, mine was my Grandma Nishimoto. She always encouraged me to write and none of this would have been possible if she hadn't inspired me from an early age.

Contents

PULL AT THE THREADS

Foreword

Tammie Oka's powerful and adept debut collection portrays a young woman's family, social and intimate relationships growing up in Hawai'i. The title of her book alludes to her Local Japanese-American heritage which layers her savvy, sexually-frank, emotionally brave poetry with a rich culture. Her combination of honesty and vernacular (pidgin and slang) makes none of the poetry heavy-going—it has lightness in its being despite the serious themes of casual intimacy, sexual abuse by a student bully, bulimia, a child in the midst of a divorce, and care for an imperfect but loving father. The serious subject matter is open to a readership concerned with healing through art; her poems, in the voicing of pain, overcome life's minor and major adversities and reach out to others. Many will identify with the sardonic passion and dismay at the weaknesses of others. Poetry aficionados will be impressed by Ms. Oka's lyrical gifts, including the finely judged line-break, the telling run-on phrase, and her command of the open-form.

Tammie Oka's obvious literary influences include Sharon Olds, Lois-Ann Yamanaka, and Denise Duhamel, and she has read widely and deeply in the poetry of the Americas and the Pacific. I believe that Ms. Oka will become an important poet of Hawai'i whose work deserves wide dissemination. I have every confidence in recommending this wonderful book.

This is the third publication by Kahuamānoa Press—its first two collections by Ann Inoshita and Sage Takehiro have established it as a reputable poetry publisher. Kahuamānoa is a terrific addition to the growing and established stable of poetry publishers in the State which include Bamboo Ridge Press, Tinfish, and Kuleana O'iwi Press.

Robert Sullivan
Director of Creative Writing, University of Hawai'i at Mānoa.

For Margaret Park Nishimoto.

This is how I keep your memory alive.

Do as Your Parents Say

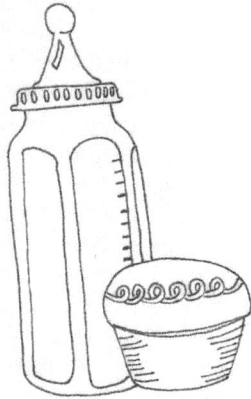

MILK STAINS

Life began on the yellow carpet flaked with skin
where stone against stone their bodies sparked.

Bottle in hand, the infant spelled her name across the fibers,
leaving traces of her mother wherever she crawled.

And the mother swore from that day she'd live for her daughter,
while the father thought she could be everything he was not.

EXPLORATION

Before she discovered
boys or brand names
the girl found her body,
learned that she could
bite all ten nails off
her ten toes.

She bent her arms
and legs in ways they
shouldn't be bent,
walked on
ceramic tiles with
the tips of her toes.

With her finger extended,
she dipped into the
wealth of her own filth,
extracted a booger
from her nose and placed
it in her mouth
to see what all the
fuss was about.

She liked the salty
sweetness. It tasted
like dried cuttlefish,
not like the sour soap
that would enter her
mouth when bathed.

She found a new use
for her hair after
watching the dentist
floss her teeth
with the soft nylon thread.

Inventive, the girl realized
that she didn't need

soap and water
to create bubbles—
saliva would suffice.

But the part of her body
she found most odd
was below her stomach,
where her skin bulged
like the cheeks of
the goldfish.

Her mother told her
it was her private
part, so she covered
it as best she could.
At night she pulled
the blanket up between
her legs.

And the more she
tugged the better
it felt, until
the day her mother
caught her flustered red.

Her mother didn't have
words to explain,
she could only tell
her daughter that
what she was doing
was bad, and hope
like everything else
it would soon pass.

Dad Said He Loved Me with Food

We made weekly, if not daily stops
to the 7-Eleven on the corner of
Beretania and Artesian,
plucked Hostess snacks
from the shelves as if a hurricane
were coming our way. But Mom

never approved of the
Ho Hos, Ding Dongs, or Cup Cakes,
so we tried to hide our stash
anywhere we could—
in the back of the fridge behind
the frozen chicken, in the cabinet
behind the pots and pans. We stood
in front of the white door, in
the shadow of coolness trying to devour
our snacks before Mom caught
us brown-handed. Dad, beer-belly
sticking out of his scrubs, needed to huddle

behind the fridge and I laughed
at the sight. We loved Cup Cakes
the most, with the curly
white frosting down the center.
They were always best with milk.

"What are the two of you doing?"
Mom asked, hearing our whispers.
"Nothing," I replied. A ring of chocolate
circled my mouth. Dad preferred me
to take the blame instead of hearing Mom
grumble, but he knew and I knew
that he'd take the fall:

"I told you not to feed her anymore
chocolate! For Christ sakes
do you want her to look like you?"

Father's Nightbird Song

In the stairwell
    Father strums his guitar,
        closes his eyes,
            takes a puff of True 100.
                Smoke transports us,
                    and we are surrounded
                        by neon lights.

Father extends his arm
    toward the dart board
        as I peel the labels
            off brown bottles.
                One more round,
                    one more Bud,
                      then we can finally
                      go home.

In the elevator,
    Father sings
        Kalapana songs
            to a stranger
                and I find him,
                    the next morning
                      with his arms
                        sprawled out,
                          over the tub
                            like a nightbird.

                fly on, fly on.

Portuguese Bean Soup

Dad

      and

          I

              were fishermen

                    in a pond full of koi.

We   h o v e r ed

      over the pot

with   ladle   in   hand,

fishing out pieces of

      ham hock

        and

                Portuguese sausage

when
Mom
wasn't
looking.

Dad and I   s m i l e d   at each other

      as Mom   e y e d   our bowls of soup.

Finders keepers, losers weepers.

"Godfunnit you two pigs!
Next time leave some meat for me,
unless you both like cook!"

HIGH CHOLESTEROL

"She needs to go on a diet,
she's overweight
and her cholesterol is 270."

"I can refer you to a dietician
Elise Matsumoto—she works
well with children."

I figured anything over 200
was bad, Dad's weight
and now my cholesterol.

Mom's face said it all.
*Poor child, say good-bye
to those Ho Hos and Ding Dongs.*

Mrs. Manatelli's Second Grade Class

On da firs day of school
my madda stood wit me
in front of da bulletin board,
and we look who my teacha was.
Second gradas, and I saw my name
unda Mrs. Manatelli.
I thought I was going drop dead
cuz all my frens
told me she one real witch
and keep one eye on everybody
cuz she follow um from
kindagarden to da second grade.

Wen I got to class
Mrs. Manatelli neva look
like one witch. She had one pointy nose,
her hair was black, but real short
like Audrey Hepburn.
She tell me wit one telephone voice
for put my backpack in da cubby hole,
and tell us for say
what we wen do during da summa.
But I neva did nuting
I just stay at my grandmadda's house,
so I lie and make up one story
and tell her I wen everywhere—
to Ice Palace and Chuck E. Cheese
almos every day, and my classmates
get stars in dere eyes cuz I know
dey wish dey could go
doz kine places every day.

My teacha not so bad. She only
get crazy wen Kai make yakamashi.
He Vietnamese or Chinese, but I cannot tell
da difference cuz dey all look da same—
like dere maddas no feed um.
I tink Kai must be poor cuz every time

he stand up I can see his ding ding.
I wonda why his parents no buy him BVDs
cuz he get one gold chain
hanging around his neck. I tink
Mrs. Manatelli like choke him
wit da chain, like my madda wen she say
she like ring my neck cuz I keep
spilling milk all ova da floor.

One time Kai no stay still
and Mrs. Manatelli got so mad
she wen get da jump ropes we use
for PE, tie him to da orange chair
and made him sit dere till we pau skool.
Kai wen shut up, but he neva cry.
I tink if Mrs. Manatelli tie me
to da chair I would cry or
make shi shi in my pants cuz
wen I come home my fadda
gone whack my okole wit da
ping pong paddle or rubba band my mout.

Mrs. Manatelli teach us
how for spell all kine words.
Today she teach us how for spell
parts of da body like
hand, arm, feet, and troat.
"You spelt everything right
except for throat. Why did you spell
throat without an 'h'?"

I try tink of one excuse
cuz I no like her
strap me to da chair like Kai.
"Sorry Mrs. Manatelli,
I cannot help—I'm part Pordagee."

THE ATLAS OF DAD'S BACK

(for the Squaw Valley poets)

Dad tell me he going give me two bucks if I scratch his back
for ten minutes. Anyting beside my allowance sound good,
so I grab da back scracha wit bear claws ready to make money.
But ten minutes turn to twenty and he says "oh pretty please" for
scratch some more. Sometime wen he stay cheap I see um
rubbing his back against da door frame until da itch stay gone.

Mom get da gross job. Dad make her pop all da pimples on his back.
She get long finga nails and I can tell she like squeezing all da
blackheads out cuz she get one grin on her face wen he scrunches
his nose and shakes his body. She tell um he one big panty
dat he cannot handle pain like wen she gave birth to me. "Look!"
He bleeding. Mom count da squiggly black worms and
tell me for use toilet paper to stop da bleeding. Dad stay hunch ova
in one ball I ask him why he no scrub betta when he go bocha.

Sometimes wen no mo nutting on TV, I tell Dad
let's play da spelling game. So he lie on his stomach like
one monk seal and I spell out words on his back. "Apple?"
Nope. Almost like he no mo sensation back dere cuz
I know he not lolo. Dad spell letters on my back. *I.* He tell me I get
    um right.
3? No. *K?* No. I give up. "Next one," he tell me. *U.*

GARDENIAS

Mother brought home gardenias
from the farmer's market.
I looked at them trying to resist the scent,
but I gave in, held them to my nose,
surrendered to memory.

"Don't go and play too far,
stay in the yard," Grandma calls.
So I occupy myself in her front yard
jump island-shaped stepping stones—
from Molokai to Maui,
to get to the gardenia bush.
I hold the white petals to my face,
take a breath of spicy sweetness.

"I don't know why dey gotta steal
my mangoes," Grandpa declares
as he peers out the window at the men
fleeing in the beat up truck.
He grabs his bucket hat,
goes into his yard with
the mango-picking pole.
I am his eyes, point at the
reddened mangoes ready to drop.

"Bring back your candy so I can check it
before you eat it," says Mom.
She saw an NBC special
about a man who stuck razors in candied apples,
doesn't trust Waipahu anymore,
so I bring home my Times bag
filled with Twix, Kit Kats, and Sixlets,
watch as she sorts through the pile on
my grandparents' living room floor.

"Look at this place," says Dad.
"The whole neighborhood is turning Filipino."
He shakes his head, reaches for the plaque

carved with our family name
hanging over the front door.
The rooms look so much smaller
without furniture, without people.
He traces his finger over the letters.
In a week, a family of six will move in.

Reverberation of Words

The parents stare at me, wondering where my child is. The nurses laugh when I answer their questions; tell them my date of birth. I sit in my pediatrician's waiting room watching *Gay, Straight, or Taken* on my iPod. At twenty-three, I'm too old to blend into the uncomfortable leather seats, so I distract myself to make time pass by, blow my nose in unison with the noise. A child playing on the game table glances at me while children from the blond-haired mother run around in circles. I turn the volume louder, but I can still hear the children yell. "Use your words," the mother tells her child.

Hey bacon!

The fat is melting off your arms.

Shamu, I like your sequel!

School was hell. Three boys would tease, kick, and beat me up at the bus stop in front of Washington Intermediate after school. Tate was the worst. He'd call me fatso and kick me until one of his friends said enough, and if no one was around he wouldn't stop.

Miss, he started it!

Not!

Both of you better quit it before I send you to the counselor's office.

But Miss, he grabbed my boob and called me—

I don't care who started it. Both of you go outside!

Mrs. Mikami didn't care who started the fight. She only wanted productivity and peace in her ceramics class.

She never listened to me when I told her Tate, Justin, and
Andrew called me names.
She never listened to me when I told her they threw pea-sized clay
balls at the back of my head.
She never listened to me when I told her that Tate groped me in class.

Stop!   **Help!**   **Somebody.**

No one hears. No one cares. He smiles as he walks away.

SURRENDER

Uncle took Kimbie and me to Hanauma Bay,
said he wanted to show us a giant-sized toilet bowl.
We walked beyond the warning signs,
moistened our tabis in pools of sea water
collected on sharp lava rocks. When
we reached Toilet Bowl, Uncle told us
to dive right in, but I stopped, watched
the haole tourists, swirling, bobbing up and down.

Uncle motioned me to hurry up as the water rose.
I took a deep breath, cannonballed into foamy white mist.
The undertow weaved into tangles of my hair,
pulled me lower as sand gathered above like clouds.
I stared at the surface, brown haze battling rays of sunlight
wondering if this is what heaven felt like:
a bear hug from Father, salt entering every part of my body.
I stopped searching for rock, surrendered
as lukewarm waters slowly caressed my skin.

THIRTEEN AGAIN

Fossilized like petals torn
from Mother's birthday bouquet,
carefully dried in the dictionary,
I open the wooden doors, pages
of my yearbook and I see his face
his name, and I am thirteen all over again.

I walk to the Ruger bus stop
on my way to Grandma's house
and he is walking beside me,
in front of me, all around me.
I sit on the concrete bench,
pray that he doesn't punch me,
pray that the bus is near.

Hey fatso. Hey Shamu.
You must really like Nik,
and I am slow to respond
because I don't want him to leave
bruises on my skin, don't
want Grandma to worry,
rush to school to rescue me
in her Chrysler Plymouth van.

I wait for the bus,
try to play along because
we are alone, and I
fear him when his friends
aren't around. My intestines
latch in knots, and he
suddenly tugs my backpack
and drags me past bushes.
I press his arms into
thorns and leaves, but I am
running in place, and no
one's around and no one answers
my screams. He opens the
gate to his apartment building,

pushes me behind the bushes
and I kick him. He pulls me
tighter, closer.

His warm breath smells like cigarettes
and his eyes go black. He stares
down at me like a man
who has gone without
food and water for days.
I know the look and cannot,
will not escape.

He unwraps me like a birthday present
under each layer of clothing—
my button-down blouse, tank top,
and white bra. I am numb. He leaves
when he has taken what he came for,
laughs as he slowly walks away.
I tug my clothes back in place. Cry,
silent for years.

I close the yearbook and gather
the dried petals, the ones I planned
to use for potpourri, stand on my lanai
nine stories above the ground
release the petals from my hands.

IN THE SHOWER WHERE DREAMS ARE MADE

FOURTH GRADE

Pour Pert Plus over the glossy white surface.
I slide left to right, water on cold
mimicking Kristy Yamaguchi in the '92 Olympics,
twirl my body in circles.
Streams of water skirt my skin—
audience, mold stains on the shower curtain,
but no one gasps when my bottom meets the floor.

SEVENTH GRADE

Belt a little louder, like the radio on full blast.
Walls echo Mariah Carey's octave range.
This is where size hasn't defied me
and my lungs spread wide.
With shampoo foam,
I run my fingers across the wall
and write lyrics on canary yellow tiles.
The words melt away
and soap stains my voice between grout.

NINTH GRADE

Turn the water on high.
I make sure no one hears a sound,
place my index and middle fingers
in the back of my throat
as I try to rid myself of myself.
Acid burns. Everything is peach.
I mash each chunk with both feet,
attempt to wash my double chin
and thick waist down the drain
because Ice Capades are for children,
and no on wants to see Shamu sing.

SHELTER

When the girl was born
her mother and father swore
they wouldn't let her suffer
the mistakes they had learned
from experience.

They fashioned a cedar box
lined with velvet and placed her in it.
Before they sealed the lid
over her fontanelle, still moist
from birth, they told her
it was for her own good
and she believed them.

They tied a satin ribbon
around the edges to make sure
she wouldn't escape—
as warning sign,
but every now and then
people, faces, names slid in.

In the fourth grade the girl came home
and told her mother that Alice said
that Joey from New Kids on the Block
spit semen onto someone in the audience
at one of their concerts. The mother
called the girl's teacher, told her the
new word her daughter learned in class,
condemned the teacher for letting
such a foul word slip into the girl's head.

Frightened that she hadn't been
more careful, the mother
stuffed cotton balls into the girl's ears
and told her not to listen to her classmates.
But the cotton balls weren't enough
since she learned new words every day
at home. One day when the father

helped the girl with her multiplication
on the dining room table, she couldn't
understand nine times nine even though
she knew each multiple of twelve,
and the girl said *shit.*

The father asked the girl where
she learned such a word,
and she replied that she had
heard him say it many times before
when he was frustrated with work
or when he made the darts bounce
off the backboard at the bar.
The father scolded the girl
and told her never to use the word again,
to do as he says and not as he does
and duct taped the girl's mouth shut
so the mother would never find out.

Each year the lid sealed tighter.
The only people let into the box
were members of her family,
and because of this the girl forged a bond
with Grandmother, her only messenger
from outside.

The girl spent days, summers
at Grandmother's house
and asked her all kinds of questions:
Why is her grandfather so grouchy?
What were her children like when
they were young? Grandmother
answered her honestly, without hesitation.
She told the girl that her grandfather
was grouchy because they hadn't had
sex in three months, that sometimes
she felt cold at night so she had to
make love with her shirt on.

Grandmother told the girl that
her uncle used to hide pot in the
light fixtures and that her mother
would always disappear for hours at
a time. The girl and Grandmother
spent nights talking about the past.
They giggled and Grandmother
let the girl borrow her clothes
and jewelry because they were
the same size. And the cedar fumes
were finally bearable.

In the summer of '97, the year the girl
transitioned to high school,
Grandmother became ill.
The girl knew the disease
had always lingered in Grandmother's lungs.
Maybe Grandmother used all her energy
to tell her the truth. She watched
her messenger slowly slip away.
First, into the IV needles,
then into the nursing home
with the shabby view of Liliha streets.

With Grandmother out of reach,
the girl collapsed into the folds
of velvet. Escorted by her mother,
she visited Grandmother several times a week.
But their eyes were the only secret connection
in the room filled with people.

When Grandmother passed, the girl
sunk deep into the box.
The mother and father had filled
her head with should nots:
You should not walk out of the house
with your shoulders bare.
You should not swear.

You should not have sex until marriage.
You should not smoke cigarettes
or do drugs.

But the girl was tired of all the
should nots with no one to tell
her the truth. She devised a plan
to get away from her parents,
told the mother and father that
the summer school program would
look good on her college application.

The mother and father obliged,
sent her off to Northwestern
with a care package to last all summer long.
There the girl felt so far from home,
free for a whole month.
She cried and wept, and found a pack
of cigarettes to calm her nerves.
Then the girls at the summer program
told her they had something that would
make her forget all her worries,
that she'd even forget her box.

They poked a hole in a plastic Pepsi bottle,
used a gum wrapper to seal the top,
told her to *toke it,* told her to *puff.*
The girl took hit after hit of the brown stuff
her mother warned her not to touch.
She counted twenty breaths. Her head spun,
legs weighed down with lead; blue, red,
and green dots blurred her vision.

When she stepped off the plane
she didn't have to say a word, the mother
could smell the weed on her clothes.
Immediately, the parents sent her back
into the box and lined her nose with
Vicks VapoRub, hammered the lid shut.

The girl clung to the velvet already
tattered with age. There she continued
to study, avoided the should nots,
watched her friends go out
as her body grew larger, taller.

She didn't attend the winterballs
or homecomings—they wouldn't
allow it. She couldn't date,
because dating would lead to sex.
So she took her computer into her box,
disguised herself in deep study,
and the internet became her best friend.
On Hawaii Chat Universe
she met a boy, then she met a man
and together they snuck out
on Fridays. He told her he loved her,
that he could rescue her.
She picked a date. Prom night.
And she told her mother a lie,
that he was twenty, and that
she'd be back before sunrise.
On the balcony of her friend's
hotel room the man asked *are you ready?*—
and she let him in as they watched
the sun rise over the railing.

The mother stayed up all night
waiting for the girl, and she knew
without speaking that the girl had
been touched. Furious, the mother
got out her biggest pot and began
to boil water. She commanded the
girl to get in, to clean herself,
and the girl got in even though the bubbles
would boil her skin. But she didn't care
because she had finally broken free
from the cedar box.

PRETEND TO BE HAPPY

My Immortal

(for grandma)

I've died this death many times before.

    The first death came
        when Mother passed.
            She was replaced by another—
                she had a husband, two children,
                    to Father
                        she was merely a mistress, concubine.
                I was the skinniest, ugliest child,
            Father felt unattached
        so out of all his children, he chose me
    to live with Mrs. Ono.

Slave
    I was her slave.
Cook and clean
    scraps were
        all I had to eat.
At night while everyone slept
    I crept into the kitchen,
        took a bite of leftovers,
            stole some bread.

When Father felt I was out of line
    he whipped out his belt,
        hung me by my head
            on the mango tree.
                I'll never forget how I clung to life
                    tugging the leather,
                        feet against the bark.

    I told myself that one day
        I would run away
            to Honolulu Harbor
                to the boats filled

with tourist hoards.
I would dive into the water
collect the coins they threw
save up for a new life

somewhere far
far from Kalihi
far from Mrs. Ono
she took every thing from me
not only my father, two houses in my name,
my strength, my youth.

The second death came when
I graduated from the eighth grade.
We were in a car,
he called it a date.
Flesh unseen,
breasts untouched,
he took my innocence.

His child
grew inside of me.
There was no turning back
so I married the man
who raped me,
who stole my youth.

After the second death
all that seemed fair
dissipated with time.
I bore three children to my husband.
Yet, it was not enough
so he hired himself whores.

This third death, I should have expected.
I could read the signs:
*Playboy*s hidden under the bed
late night plumbing jobs, bar stops,

still I figured these were manly devices
until one day when he brought home
another woman.
               He kissed her in front of me.
I closed my eyes, locked myself in my room.

Hardship was not enough
    I saw my fourth death in the eyes of my only daughter.
        Like me, beaten by her father
           the Dragon King,
               she went through life spineless,
                  the same miseries—
                      three marriages, I never approved.
              The first committed adultery
          the second compared her to his ex
      the third at least gave her a child,
    the flame of her eye.
  Like fate to the fire
the perpetuated cycle
    her child, another girl
        more problems.
              Don't let her be like us
                 she was destined for more.

So I told my granddaughter she was special
           she was unlike me or her mother;
she could read and write so well.
    One day I know she'll write our stories
choose a different life,
    complete her education.

So with my fifth and final death I'll give her
    all the strength I have built
        throughout the years.

I'll give her all my hopes, my dreams
I'll give her the power to conquer the world of man
I'll give her voice and show her how to scream.

So as I lie here,
    Kuakini my final resting place
        my granddaughter whispers in my ear,

"It's okay Grandma, you can go now
you don't have to fight anymore
just remember to visit me in my dreams."

    On Benken's sea
        I ride on ribbons of
            blue, green, and purple.

        I am coming home today
the clouds look heavy.

I am the jellyfish
    passing on my sting
        where her mother and I have faltered

        my granddaughter will be the first to rise above.

I Should Have

I can almost see your faces
in a pot of broth.

        I can almost hear laughter
        in crackling oil on the stove.

            I can almost smell grandmother
            in the parsley mixed with rose-scented soap.

                I remember you both
                with each breath
                pray I remember.

        Mom tries

      senses fade

    only pictures
remain.

Best Friends Forever

"Stupid, stop wasting my stog!
Just keep the smoke in your mouth.
You have to inhale, and stop holding it
like a joint before security comes."
I let the cigarette dangle between
my index and middle fingers
choked, coughed, held the smoke in
like a mist of marijuana
as Ty stood over me laughing.
Each day I trained my lungs to breathe,
tricked hunger with oral fixation.

"You're giving me a headache.
Stop pressing on the brakes!"
Ty let me drive his mom's Saturn
in circles around Market City parking lot
and I drove up and down the asphalt
because my parents never trusted me
behind the wheel. He taught me
to brake, then accelerate on turns
and I made the backseats drop
with sudden stomps.

"You ready?"
Ty taught me what hands do
in a tent at Kahana Bay.
We lay next to each other
under stars, drunk off Bud Light.
But I wasn't ready because the scent
of salt water still lingered in my hair
and I wanted to mask the smell
of bathing suit showers,
so I grabbed a Massengill towelette
to prepare for his entrance.
With his fingers, he jabbed into me
with jackhammer motions.
I wondered if sex would be just as bad.

"You wanna go to Fusions?"
I hadn't seen Ty in years
because after high school we parted,
went on separate paths, and under
neon lights, the sequin glares
emanating from busty men
it all made sense—
his perfectly groomed eyebrows,
matching outfits, and feminine gestures.
And though he was my first in so many ways
I understood why we never made it.

Dat Kine Advice

How come you come to me for dat kine advice?
You want one prom date so you wen look on da intanet,
and he stay how old?
Ho, you fuck'n crazy I tell you, yeah
you betta tell your parents he only twenty cuz
if not, you know dey gone kick your okole
and betta yet da bugga Filipino.
What you trying for do, give your fadda one heart attack?
What, you no like Japaneez?
Why, cuz dey get pinky-size boto?

So dats what you like, you wanna know
how for give da twenty-six year-old one blow job.
You gotta lick um up and down and no use pleny teeth
if not, sowa, and you no like make him sowa
cuz den he gone know you one virgin.
No forget da balls, dey dere for one reason.
Gotta play with um like da silva balls from Chinatown
and no squeeze too hard, bumbai da bugga gone
slap you in da head.

You so fuck'n crazy I tell you, if you just
stop shoving doz goddamn Ho Hos in your face
den someone take you prom—aye, no forget use rubbas
if not your madda gone get real mad wen you
get hapai wit one mutt and you gotta get one abortion
and have da machine suck um out
cuz you no can handle pain, cuz sowa la dat.

What you mean how I know? Cuz I know.
What you tink dis Sunday church confessional?
Stupid I tell you, all cuz you get one picture of
da dress you like in your head.
I thought you smart, but you real lolo
if you tink he really like get to know you.
No come to me for advice anymore
stupid fuck'n Japanee, you already get
everyting in the goddamn world.

How to Be a Good Ojoosan

earn a's
graduate with honors
go to law school
don't swear
listen to your parents
don't answer back
eat mochi
boil s & s ramen
shop at times supermarket
go to shinnyoen
dress conservatively
cross your legs
vote for daniel inouye
take off shoes before entering
always refuse offers three times
take japanese
drive a toyota corolla
use salux bathing cloths
learn to bon dance
visit the motherland
buy omiyage before trips
go to disneyland and las vegas
listen to hip hop and r & b
play taiko drums
go out with someone japanese
wait until marriage
marry rich
have children
don't shame the family
live in pearl city
wear slippers
visit ancestors' graves
pour shoyu over rice
put family first
make a family crest out of cranes
send thank you cards
let your husband wear the pants
pretend to be happy

earn an mfa
become a writer
say fuck shit bitch asshole
tell your father to fuck off
try different ethnic foods
like gyros, pho, and chow mein
get a taste of the world
don't go to church
to listen to *nam yo ho ren ge kyo*
and clanging bells
wear cleavage-baring tops
and mini skirts
vote liberal
wear your shoes on the carpet
say yes yes yes
learn spanish so you can say *como mierda*
swear in several tongues
drive a bmw
learn to bump and grind on the dance floor
take trips across the atlantic
to paris, london, and madrid
listen to alternative rock and indie music
turn save ferris on full blast
use yasmin and nuva ring
so you won't get knocked up
at an early age
be promiscuous
fuck a puerto rican man
to make your father proud
move to seattle
wear trench coats and black makeup
visit bruce lee's grave
change your last name
live on broadway between pike and pine
trade in rice for pasta
send postcards to your family
find sweetness in your own reflection
in puddles of water in the rain

POSTCARDS

LONDON, UK

Antique silver spoons jangle on Portobello Road.
April mist draws cotton candy circles on morning cheeks.
Ché Guevara looks down from the tube overpass
greeted by scents of sausage and tulips,
coating the air like cough syrup
and realize this is the furthest I've ever been from home.

NEW YORK, NY

Yellow cabs honk, weave in and out of traffic;
New York City planned from the pages of *Fodor's*.
Broadway drips of tourist souvenirs,
smells like noodle cakes and fresh bread.
I am outside Pearl River Mart
holding a bag filled with Chinese slippers
I'll never use, except to stare at
in contentment
because I saw them on the internet.
I light a cigarette
the city stops, slows down—
picture perfect postcard.
I pick up my cell phone,
call Chris because I've dreamed
of visiting the Big Apple all my life.

EVANSTON, IL

Lake Michigan lies in silence
on the shores of Evanston, with
a rickety white picket fence;
the lifeguard chair stands alone.
I swim out, far out
no current to battle
no creatures to carry me under.
I could never swim so far out into the Pacific.

SEATTLE, WA

Grey shadows the weary town
jet blasted by rain and cold.
I leave the window open in my dorm room.
It feels like air-conditioning—thirty degrees outside.
I walk down Broadway, turn on Pike,
pass the twenty-somethings dressed in black,
last minute Christmas shopping
before heading home for good.
I stand in front of Bon Marché.
Christmas lights, a star and angels dangle
eight stories high, and for the first time
it feels like Christmas as I stand here
wrapped up in a winter coat.

HONOLULU, HI

The bronze rays are so consistent.
I could set my watch by sunrise and sundown.
People hold doors open
say aloha, mahalo
sand trails me wherever I go, and I am home
jump on my bed
with the fan in my face, set on high.

Morning Sex

You grope my thighs
eyes adjusting to sunlight seeping
through frosted window panes.

    I turn right, so your five o'clock shadow
        brushes my back.
            You shuffle off blankets and underwear,
               arrange our bodies like spoons
                   because in light we cannot face each other.

The stench of last night
still radiates from our mouths,

               but anticipation intensifies with motion
             toes curl, I press nails into your arms.

Three-hundred-thread count turns to ocean.
We create waves, like breath
rippling across a cup of coffee.

        You turn to me in silence
            because you know better than to speak.

We cannot hide four years
all our imperfections, yet in this moment
when you release yourself inside of me
bones realign.

        As you search for something to wipe me from your body

           I lie here, trying to hold you in.

BORROWING THINGS

I hate borrowing things.
I borrow books.
The library sends me a bill
for $10.

I borrow a DVD.
Blockbuster tells me
I can buy the movie
for full-price after 30 days.

I borrow a cell phone.
Chris tells me
to keep the conversation short
because he's over his minutes.

I borrowed you
when my lover found someone else.
He showed me his lighter
etched with his and her names
as proof.

I lost myself between your sheets,
your arms, your legs,
but now I must return you
after one night—
the alcohol and weed
have worn off
and now I realize
all you wanted was a good fuck.

My lover calls me the next day
says he's sorry, says he wants
me back.
I go to my computer, check
my e-mail. Damn!
Even my credit card payment
is past due.

ODE ON A RAZOR

The bathroom light shadows
your elliptical face, and in
the lower hemisphere
my hands trace angles—
a path for the decadent razor,
deforestation of black pine and grass.
With your visage in plain view,
I nudge the plateau
above your lips,
kiss the soft stubbles
below your chin—
those places I love,
rough and gentle
those mornings when I'm
melded to your skin.

The Stripper's Guide to Looking Great Naked
declares I have an "O" shape,
so I spread wide, with Mach 3 razor in hand.
I focus, not to knick.
It's supposed to shave closer
make you want me.
Three-tiered blade
runs perpendicular
to clam lips.
Maybe the watermelon-color will
remind you of those nights
blindfolded, handcuffed,
steam on your windshield.
The landing strip goes great
with chunky thighs
it'll guide you home.

When denial fails
intuition is a curse.
I should've known
those late-night trips, those calls
you didn't utter my name,
now I stand here
in front of the mirror,
open a new cartridge
three layers of sharp
to trickle the pain.
I run the blade vertically
press the handle further,
crimson drips from my arms.
What kills is the silence. Hush.

APHRODITE SEES A PSYCHIATRIST

Dr. Kosaki
        says that men don't change.
                "So forget Adonis, live with Hephaestus."

She says it was
        one night, a one night stand.
                I must purge him from my memory.
                        The dosage of Prozac
              cannot be increased
        medicine was never meant to cure
pining, loneliness, this pain.

"Work with me," she pleads.
    I try to forget.

I try to forget his spiky hair
wanting to run my fingers through them.
      I try to forget those parties
      I always stared at him from across the room.
          I try to forget the chill rising up my back
          the feel of his arm against me.
              I try to forget those drives around Kapalono Park
              searching for his house, his car
              childish case of cat and mouse.
                  I try to forget his conversations.
                  I always knew he was wise.
                  Hephaestus never understood politics.
                      I try to forget stopping at his workplace.
                    Why did I always prefer Papa Johns?
                        I try to forget his car:
                        purplish Civic
                        stickers plastered to the sides.

                  "Stop," she says,
              "You cannot cling to the good
          remember the bad
        number them one by one

repeat them over in your head
it's the only way to let go of the past.
What would others think
with their goddess of love
seeing a shrink?"

So I try to remember the bad
on my trips down from Olympus.

I remember he could never go
without
weed
pakalolo
aunty
mary jane

I remember he turned red—
a mortal thermometer.

Japanese boys were never meant to drink.

I remember what he said.
He dumped all of his girlfriends
even so, I still would take the chance.

She tries to snap me out of it.
I go back to that night
once again, I try to abide
try to erase the drunken memory

four Coronas
two Midori sours
rum, Coke, and
Jaegerbomb.

If I could just forget that one night
maybe I could return to Hephaestus
be happy, never want to touch that supple skin.

I try to forget him undressing.
I try to forget his red boxers.
I try to forget the way he shivered
    as I leaned over him.
I try to forget him unzipping
    my pants.
I try to forget his body, naked
    my sexual fantasies finally reality.
I try to forget the way he felt
    wedged between my legs.
I try to forget the panting, the moans.
I try to forget never finishing
    what we had started
    now I'm certain alcohol and weed
    just don't go together.
I try to forget how innocent
    he looked in his sleep.
I try to forget the curve of his cheeks;
    his body was perfect.
I try to forget the way he tugged at me
    in the land of dreams.
I try to forget the good-byes we said
    the morning he dropped me off
    at the foot of my mountain
    sadness loomed overhead.

    Adonis, he did not know what to do
        knowledge in matters
            left to the goddess of love.

I kissed his cheek.
        He patted my head.
            I'll try to forget that one night
                more than a one night stand.

Adonis will always be my second
      enraptured, my heart
         my first,
and if he decided to climb Olympus
      I would not refuse
         to leave the life I have come to know,
           Hephaestus, Eros.
             Even goddesses have no power over
               a heart longing for a mortal soul.

SATAN SPEAKS TO ME OF REVENGE

He whispers in my ear
that revenge is honest
it coats the tongue with rusted iron
because in this world there is
no Joseph   no Jesus   no Mary   no God
to save me and when the junkie high on ice
jimmies open my car door
and steals my books
instead of taking quarters from my ashtray
I want to find him
cut off his hands
and watch blood splatter
across the bindings but I can't
so I envision each page
slicing open his hands
and the memory of him melts away

and when my boss tells me
she has no sympathy for us folk
who serve fast-food re-heated food
piece-of-shit food to customers
I glance down at her pregnant belly
and I can already see the result
stupidity multiplied
and Satan tells me to collect turds
from cat litter and watch her eat
each drop of stool   toxoplasmosis
the sentiments are the same
I have no sympathy because revenge
is honest and sympathy makes you weak

and Satan tells me to help him out
so to the lover who viciously hurt me
when he least expects it when he thinks
I've forgiven him for his infidelities

fuck him fuck his friend to fuck him
because revenge is honest and God
doesn't believe in a good fuck
but I've been in Satan's bed
and he knows how to make me come.

CONVINCE YOURSELF

You don't love him.
Cut off four inches
and dye your hair black
because love is
two letters short of evolve,
and when you strut into
the bar to meet your
best friend and ask her
what she thinks
she sighs Hhhhmmm
which really means
you look the same.

But you don't care
you have a new
outlook on life.
You visit your psychiatrist
just to hear the words
just to hear her say
you're not crazy when you
can't believe a word
she says.

Slide in bed with the guy
you've been eyeing for months,
besides the two of you
are ~~good~~ decent friends
and he hasn't slept around
that much.
Climb on top of him,
show him who's in charge.
Besides you shaved it
all off thinking you were
going to get some.

But now it feels awkward
you had to say hello
to his mom
on the way to his room.
You're too uncomfortable
to fuck naked,
so you leave on your top,
moan uh uh uh
even though you can't
figure out whether he's
inside you and you watch
as he goes limp like
overcooked asparagus.

You return home convinced,
grab the picture off the mirror,
shred it because
you are finally over him.
And when you realize
you lost the negatives,
tore the only picture,
you scramble to find the
pieces beside your bed.

Make Believe

You spend hours over me,
    working your hands.

        I close my eyes,
        to stay in the moment, to keep

                my mind from drifting away.

        But I still see his face, his jet black hair
      over your body as you mimic
    some new position you saw on DVD,

brought back to that night
when his body quivered in bed.
He didn't know whether to hold me,
to touch me, so I crawled toward him

      stripped away months of anticipation,

        unbuttoned his denim pants,

          kissed his thin lips.

Once—we melded to each other
in the morning light.
The odorless taste of his body
burns my memory.

      You look into my eyes—
        as I grind my body into your pelvis,
          and you ask me why I never come.

STALE AIR

We don't have conversations about the past,
it brings up too many questions
when we've worked so hard to get to this place,
this calm silence, fogged by cigarette smoke
and shady neon lights.

I stare at you as you thumb through pages
of car ads, sip MGD,
and smile to yourself in simple delight.
I want to say something, but we've exhausted speech.
You don't understand politics
and I couldn't give a shit about horsepower.

I shift my weight. The condensation from my skin is
suctioning me to the vinyl seat,
makes the wait seem longer, more uncomfortable.

The waiter arrives. You tear into
your food, use your fingers to grab
a piece of steak and I cringe,
slide the fork toward you. The meal separates us
even further, like our talks about having kids.

We've been stuck in the same diner—
wooden fans revolving overhead.
We don't go anywhere, because
we're too different, too scared to admit it,
so we sit here in contemplative silence
pretending we'll move further,
because tomorrow hasn't come.

I buy every issue of *In Style Wedding* magazine
and you get a credit card so that one day
we'll be able to rent a car when we go on a trip.
But in the back of my mind, whenever you have
that far off look, I still wonder if she was worth it
and you still want to know his name.

UGLY MEN, PRETTY WOMEN

They come into my restaurant every now and then—the men with matted grey hair and their pretty wives. The men—their stomachs protrude past their manhood. They let themselves go years ago, before they met their ex-wives and the daughters of their ex-wives. They've traded in looks for high-power jobs. They don't need to search Match.com for would-be suitors. The women seek them out, or so they think. These ugly men hold their wives' hands like the Louis Vuitton purses their wives clutch to their chest for protection. They remember what it was like to scan the racks of Forever 21 before they knew Neiman Marcus was a department store, not a man's name. The pretty women look my age. They smile at me with their Brite Smile teeth, like somehow they know what it's like to waitress, like somehow they know my pain. Their ugly husbands bought them over with the three-carat promise ring. Till death do us part; the women know their husbands will be the first to go. I tell the ugly men that they're lucky their wives are so pretty, but even I know, regardless of plastic surgery, their looks will fade. These pretty women have never known what it is to be ugly. They take on motherhood like an obstacle course; rub the Palmer's Cocoa Butter on their bellies hoping it'll obliterate every mark, every scar. When the nine months are over, they take up yoga and Pilates, charge the instant tan to their husbands' black American Express cards. At night the husbands mount themselves on top of their wives, and their pretty wives squirm for breath. Their wives take trips to Borders, to the self-help section to purchase *The Cosmo Kama Sutra*. At night, these pretty wives put on their Victoria's Secret teddies, position themselves doggy style, tell the men it's tighter back there—anything to get the men from off the top. And the ugly men come and come and their pretty wives become pregnant again, which doesn't make much sense because didn't they do it from behind? The pretty wives cry at night, to go through the routine one more time. Why couldn't they be like Holly begging Hef for a baby instead of the other way around? Now the smell of shit follows the pretty women. They've stretched their bodies past the point of their youth. They watch their young ones nip at their breasts like their husbands at night, dream of the beat up Ford pickup truck they once owned and buying generic brand. And I am glad I was never pretty like them.

PULL AT THE THREADS

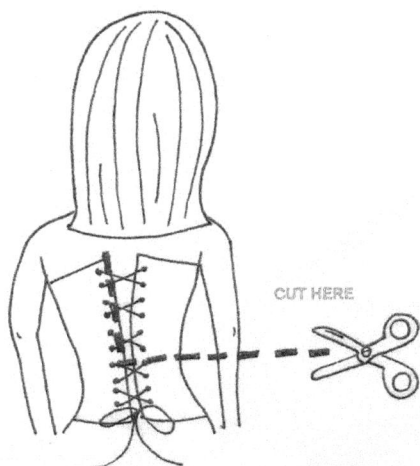

AGAINST THE INEVITABLE

She wipes each tile and crevice,
shoulder-length hair held in place
with a rhinestone barrette.
Damp honey-colored curls
cling to moist skin.

There is a softness to her
as old age slowly creeps in.
She wrings her hands
tired of circular motion.
Osteoporosis, arthritis, she wonders
if Alzheimer's is next.

She moves in and out of view
behind the opaque shower curtain.
Breasts direct eyes toward the stomach,
where motherhood once bit her.

Beads of water cling to love handles.
Time dimples thighs and backside,
places where her lovers once touched.

She catches a glance of her own reflection
on the bathtub floor, stares for a minute
and continues to dry the residual water
to keep her bathtub mildew-free.

MOVING DAY

Dad packed nineteen years into boxes,
called all his friends to help him move
his favorite love seat out of our apartment.
Mom let him stay until the divorce was final.
He couldn't bring himself to move back in
with his mother. He bought an apartment across
the freeway from our house because he
said it was closer to his workplace. Then Dad paid
for a new phone number a digit away from ours so
I wouldn't forget. *See how easy it is to remember?*

Dad packed nineteen years into boxes
and left me everything he thought I needed—
the photo albums with pictures from trips
to Disneyland, the Japanese dictionary,
and the computer. He shook hands with all
his friends, thanked them for moving what little
he had to take. I watched him wave good-bye
from the company truck as he glanced back for
one last view. When Dad got to his new
apartment he called and told me to step outside,
to look for him on his lanai. I counted the floors
of his condo and laughed. *I can always find you.*

Dad packed nineteen years into boxes
while Mom cut him out of photographs.
Now she stands alone in her off-white
wedding dress, clutching her autumn bouquet
for dear life—the lone mother with baby in arms.
She told me she wanted to change the carpets.
She ripped out tiles in the bathroom instead.
Mom bought a Bed-In-A-Bag to cover her bare mattress.
All I wanted was to give you a normal life.

STRAWBERRY JAM

The Chinese man with grandfather glasses
comes in every Saturday. I roll my eyes.
He tells me the same order with the same requests:

> broiled salmon,
> > brown rice,
> > > a side of miso sauce,
> > > > and a dinner roll with
> > > > > strawberry jam instead of butter.

He's watching his diet, tells me fish
is good for his health, places vitamin tablets
next to the glass of water.

I come back to his table, tell him we're
out of strawberry jam, ask if he wants
grape or apple. He complains as usual.

> The fish is over-cooked.
> > The prices keep on going up.
> > > Guess he'll have to eat the dinner roll dry.

He prefers the thirty-something-year-old
waitresses with kids, the ones that will sigh
along with him in discontent
thinking he might leave an extra dollar.

I keep looking at my watch at five o'clock
even though he hasn't come in months.
I wonder if he has passed on
with no one to talk to, to listen to his complaints.

> There are no special requests for fish,

> > now the fresh salmon is casketed beside him

> > > in refrigerated remains.

My Space

I painted the walls blue
        to remind myself
                that womanhood does not come packaged
                        in a pink paper box.
                                I remove the ribbon
                        from my eyes, and though
                "Genesis" says I am only a fragment
        of man, there are caverns of a woman
where man has

no room
no space
no place
to grow.

They've paced me ten seconds behind your feet
        declared us fragile creatures
                to be supported with wire, metal
        corsets and bras,
                but I prefer to be unbound
        with my tits dangling
                towards the floor
        like your phallus hung low,
                but this is where we differ in

                        sexuality
                        and more.

When you are excited
        you rise like the needle of a compass
                pointed north, and I let you think that
                        the humidity within my chambers
                                is some making of your creation,
                                        puzzle filled with your missing piece,
                                                but in the tunnel between my legs

                                        I have
                                        room
                                        space
                                        place
                                        to grow.

Though it takes half of you
                for the flower to bloom, the seed
                                has been hidden within these hands since 1973

and with choice
this is where the line is drawn.

It all started with Norma McCorvey
        a.k.a. Jane Roe—
                        third unwanted pregnancy, as Justice
        blindly tipped her scale
        allowing women the right
                        to let the seed grow within their womb
                        or to rid the space, a decision

                        that you, as man, will never have to make.

Three decades have passed.
        Justice, her dress worn thin,
                her arms tire with the weight of the scale, sword

held, arched out
against foe
against Rehnquist, White, Scalia, and Thomas.

                                They would turn the tide
                overturn Roe v. Wade.
                To them the *Constitution* does not uphold

privacy, our health,
our right to choose.

See, I never mentioned
        the reason for
                tattered edges, Justice's dress—
                        Jesus is pulling on the threads.
                        As science evolves
                        man stands idle, picks fights with pills.
                I wait in line at the counter
        seventy-two hours
Plan B to abortion

to rid
you
from the space inside of me

because

you

will not

cannot

take the space

fill the void

in places inside of me

as long as Justice stands tall
        spreads her curtains
                wide for all to see,

and though I'm made of your rib
I can abort your sons, which
                        makes me soar
                        ten seconds in front of you

                        as you gribble on blue dust behind me.

Last Night I Slept with Satan

He came to me dressed in a white suit
with glossy Florsheim shoes.
His salt and pepper hair was slicked back
and though I wouldn't normally find
his age, his looks appealing,
he looked at me with bloodshot eyes,
clasped my hand, said *ti amo,*
enchanted me with his words.

I lay next to Satan in my grandmother's bed,
rubbed my nose between strands
of his hair, calmed by the smell of VO5.
He kissed the curve of my neck,
wrapped his lanky arms around me,
engulfed me like a Persian rug.

This morning he was gone.
No crème de menthe on the pillow.
No strand of hair or flake of skin
to validate his stay, just an itch
between my legs. When I went to shower,
pulled off my underwear,
cashews and diced peanuts
flowed from my vagina onto the floor
until the pile was inches tall.
There in the middle of the stack was
a severed index finger, yellow-nailed,
pointing at me in contempt.

RUSH TO LONGS DRUGS AT 2 A.M.

You're past due,
over a week,
and every time you
sit on the toilet
you pray that
the two-ply will
suddenly register red.

Just a smudge,
a dot to mark
twenty-eight days,
to know that
you haven't
destroyed your life.

Besides, the OBGYN
has you on
Ortho Tri-Cyclen
even though
every now and then
you forget
a pill or two,
and against
recommendations
decide to down
three pills instead of
using backup
protection.

You search through
the yellow pages
thinking of the worst
scenario. There in
big bold letters, under
abortion services,
are words that
would scare
your mother—
Planned Parenthood.

She doesn't want
a bastard for her
first grandchild.

But you've always been
tragic, pessimistic
at best. You put down
the phone book,
collect yourself,
and rush to Longs Drugs.

It's two in the morning.
All the grandmas
and on-lookers
are asleep in their beds.
You pick up
a First Response
double pack, thinking
you'll make a mistake.

With your legs
spread wide you pee
onto the wick,
wait two minutes
for the results to appear.
You breathe in, relieved.
Tonight you'll sleep easy.

Morning rises as if
nothing happened
and when you
see the water
sprinkled with
dark red anemones
you're thankful
for the blood, for the
constipated cramps,
and the sale
on Tampax Pearl,
aisle twelve.

STAY

Mom's not like me
she's always on the go.
On weekends she needs
to get out of the house,
go to lunch with friends,
go shopping, spend $300
on clothes.

She calls me,
tells me to call her
if I want to go out,
but I don't call
because I'd rather
stay home and rest
my sore feet
and tired smile.

I'm satisfied at home.
I flip through
channels of reality TV,
sit at my computer,
check e-mail,
and edit my webpage.

I search
the classifieds:
Manoa-Punahou-University
partly furnished studio,
no parking, $650
a month.

I want to go,
but she has gone through
too many men
too many marriages,
needs me to stay.

Finding Sanity

She eats the whole box
of Godiva chocolates,
swallows each marble.

YEARBOOK NOSTALGIA

One hundred seventy-six pages are buried
      in the closet next to *Rammstein,* and
the *Queen of the Damned* soundtrack.
       I open the puffy cover, unforgettable scribble

grow back your eyebrows
make sure your tits don't sag
I know you'll love Seattle

next to

have a great summer
have a great life
it was nice getting to know you

and I scan through senior pictures,
      my ridiculous shoulder-length hair
         curled at the ends,
            and I realize how unnatural everyone looks
               trying to give one final lasting impression.

In the row above me, my best friend Ty
      is dressed in a GAP snow jacket,
although he knew it would never snow.
      He wanted to look different
made sure he gelled his hair,
      put all five earrings on.

Then there are the local girls
      with tanned skin and Hawaiian bracelets
         dangling from their wrists.
            They remembered to place the flower accordingly:

            right ear if single, left ear if taken.
            Smile with just enough teeth.

Though it's only been four years,
I am taken back to the days I have tried to erase

newswriter, photographer, paddler, preschool volunteer

everything I once was, but I realize
everyone has changed.

Most of the pretty girls got pregnant post-graduation.
Most of the prom court never made it past the twelfth grade.
Now they're all working at the mall, in retail
and I wonder if they ever flip through the pages

reminisce with the same horror.

may all your dreams come true

don't forget me if you ever become a famous writer, or something

I smile, glance at my *Writer's Digest*
and poetry books carpeting the floor.

What I Learned While Watching Grey's Anatomy

How many times have I held my breath under water
contemplating how much easier it would be
if I could just disappear? They'd call it a mistake.
She must've drowned in the bathtub. Maybe she slipped
and knocked her head on something hard.

Meredith admitted in the place between heaven and now
that she'd let go, just for a minute because she was never
good enough for her mother. She was no more than ordinary.
And isn't that what we are taught to fear from a young age?

Dad always told me I had to be more than him. His father
wanted him to be a doctor and he had failed,
opted for a field that didn't require an MD. He saves lives,
watches newborns breathe for the first time in his hands.
But when he places the mums on the column barium, his
    achievements
and the respiratory care pin aren't enough; he can still feel the yaito
    on his hand.

Before she died, my grandmother told me that's what they did
    wrong,
pushed too hard, didn't say I love you enough.
She marks my height on the closet door next to Dad's lines,
tucks me into his old bed, and whispers "I love you."

And Dad shakes his head as I disappoint him one more time,
tell him that I'm tired of school, that I want to take a year off.
He liked the prospect of law school when I told him I took the
    LSATs twice.
He would've paid for my education if I went on, but that's the
    problem—
speaking about the present in past tense.

I don't want a dream sequence. I don't want my Dennys or Dylans
to tell me I'm dark and twisty, that I would've survived if only I had

put up a fight. Jacob is still optimistic, thinks he'd be a great father, tells me he wants to keep our baby if I ever become pregnant.

Then there is you, Dad. How many times have I reached out for you like Meredith to Ellis? But you don't have Alzheimer's, remember all my flaws—never getting my mathematics right, leaving Seattle after only one semester.

At my grandfather's seven-year memorial service, my relatives ask me what I'm doing, how goes my life? I tell them I'm still in college, that I'll be graduating with an MA this spring. My uncle tells me my grandfather would've been proud if he were alive, that he always wanted one of his children to go to graduate school. That is all I need to hear, all I need to know, and to you I must be anything but
    ordinary.

About the Author

Tammie Oka was born and raised in Honolulu. She has been published in *Trout Online Journal of Arts and Literature* and has a forthcoming publication in the *Hawaii Review*. She graduated from the University of Hawaii at Manoa with a Master's degree in English with a creative writing concentration in May 2007. She also has a Bachelor's degree in English and journalism. She was a recipient of the Myrle Clark Award for creative writing in 2005 and is a member of the Squaw Valley Community of Writers. This is her first book of poems.

www.ingramcontent.com/pod-product-compliance
Lightning Source LLC
Chambersburg PA
CBHW051849040426

42447CB00006B/765